Macramé for Beginners

All the Basics of Macramé at Your Fingertips

By
CARLY POWERS

CONTENTS

CHAPTER 3:
TIPS AND TRICKS   26

CHAPTER 4:
DIY PROJECTS   40

CHAPTER 5:
FREQUENTLY ASKED QUESTIONS 91

INTRODUCTION

Macramé is a textile-making process that involves the use of knots to make a variety of textiles. Since Macramé has regained widespread popularity in recent years, artisans and artists have developed inventive ways to expand the use of this art form beyond the traditional wall hangings and plant hangers.

For thousands of years, this age-old ritual has fluctuated in popularity. However, this technique will always be used to some extent due to its practicality. Just by using your hands and a few basic supplies, you can create objects like key chains and table runners.

Macramé is experiencing a renaissance, but it is not the first time. When the majority of people think about Macramé, they envision bohemian-inspired wall hangings from the 1960s and 1970s. To trace the method's roots, some argue that knotting emerged in the 13th century. According to some historians, the ancient Babylonians and Persians used knotting in artifacts dating from the early BC century centuries.

Macramé was an art form brought to the west from the Arabian nations throughout contemporary history. Weavers from this region of the world used a variety of knotting techniques to embellish the fringed edges of rugs, woven tapestries, and shawls.

Due to the widespread distribution of these textiles throughout Europe, an overwhelming number of individuals began experimenting with knotting as leisure. By the seventeenth century, the method had spread to England, where it was taught to ladies in waiting in service of Queen Mary II.

Women were not the only ones who used Macramé. Sailors knotted for practical reasons, but on lengthy trips, knotting became a way to keep themselves occupied and avoid boredom. These sailors ultimately contributed to the dissemination of this art form throughout Europe. When they reached new ports, they became merchants, trading the Macramé products they manufactured on the ship. Hammocks, belts, and caps were all popular products.

Victorians eventually began knotting textiles in the eighteenth and nineteenth centuries, but the practice was abandoned following the Industrial Revolution. Hand-knotting regained popularity in the late 1960s and 1970s but swiftly fell out of favor in the 1980s.

Combining boho and minimalism creates to create a cozy yet stylish aesthetic.

Even if you are new to Macramé or have always been familiar with it but need to reintroduce yourself, this book will prove very useful. This centuries-old practice has bounced in and out of mainstream use for hundreds of years. Nonetheless, this will always exist in some form due to its use. You can manufacture table runners and key chains with only your fingers and a few affordable materials.

Discover a fresh approach to the traditional craft of macramé, a talent practice that soared in popularity during the 1970s and is currently experiencing a renaissance. Macramé projects are the best way to bring the recent trend for luxurious, bohemian décor into your home.

CHAPTER 1:
HOW TO MACRAMÉ?

Macramé is an easy-to-learn beautiful knotting technique that anyone can master with a bit of practice! It's an excellent method to produce beautiful and functional works of art to add a vintage flair to your house.

1.1 Get Started with Macramé

A lot of practice and some Macramé cord is all you need to start making things with this technique. Macramé is a simple craft to master! Although it may appear sophisticated at first glance, it is a straightforward craft everyone can master. Once you've got the fundamental Macramé knots, you can merge them into any design you can imagine.

1.2 Important Macramé Terms

Before we begin, let's review a few Macramé words that you'll need to understand:

- **Macramé String:** It is extremely soft, has a single twist, and is most frequently made of cotton. It creates an exquisite fringe and is ideal for wall hangings. I'm unsure about using it for plant hangers. It is not very forgiving when it comes to reworking, so use caution if you find yourself untying and retying it frequently.

- **Macramé rope:** Typically, three cotton strands are twisted together. It's more durable than string and not quite as soft, but it's ideal for building plant hangers.

- **Filler Cord:** The cord or bundle of cords around which you tie the knots. Also known as inner cords or center cords.

- **Novelty Buttons:** Buttons in a range of interesting shapes.

- They are frequently used for beads when decorating jewelry and other little Macramé creations.

- **Working Cord:** The pair of cords or cords on which you are tying the knots. These are often the outside cords.

- **Reverse Larks Head:** Because it resembles a Double Half Hitch. The Larks Head knot is frequently reversed so that the back faces forward. When both knots are in the same place this technique is used when both knots are in the same place. Also, Half Hitches may be occasionally installed.

- **Spiral:** A knotted pattern with twisted elevated portions. Spiral Stitching is a popular knotting technique for Macramé plant hangers.

- **Picots:** Loops that protrude from the edges of specific knot designs. In the late 1800s and early 1900s, picot designs were prominent in Macramé creations.

- **Standing End:** This is an essential term in the world of Macramé. This term is used to indicate the tip of a cord that has been secured but not utilized to make the knot.

- **Vintage Knots:** Some Macramé knots have been used since the early 1900s or earlier and are therefore called vintage.

- **Unravel:** To cut a cable into individual fibers. As soon as a cord is cut, this will happen on its own, which is why you should always have extra cords on hand. Untangling and brushing out wires is sometimes done on purpose.

- **Stitch:** Old-school Macramé term is still in use today. In the late 1800s and early 1900s, the word "Stitch" was used to designate specific knots.

- **Weave:** In Macramé, these names are used to describe steps in which you alternate under and over cords to make a knot or design.

- **Sennit:** A collection of consecutively worked knots arranged into a column.

- **Project Board:** You can make a project board out of wire or foam, cardboard, or other materials for Macramé. Keeping the pins in place is its primary function.

- **Vertical:** Patterns or knots that are arranged vertically instead of horizontally. Most projects are built from top to bottom, also known as vertically.

- **Symmetry:** Equal designs on both sides or on the top or bottom.

- Working Cord: This is the most critical of all the Macramé terms in the Dictionary. It is the term used to describe the cord (or cords) used to tie the knots. Also referred to as a "knotting cord." They are often the outside cords.

- **Square Knot:** It's the decorative knot most usually used in Macramé creations. The Square Knot can be used to create various patterns, including alternating motifs and sennits.

- **Mounting (or to Mount):** When the cords are linked to a ring, dowel, handbag handle, jewelry clasp, or another cord, this is the initial stage of a Macramé craft.

- **Mat:** When tightened, a type of knot that is totally or partially filled in. It is typically constructed with two or more cords.

- **Braid/Plait:** terms that are used to describe designs created by crossing and weaving several threads.

- **Body:** The main area of a Macramé creation is the body.

- **Working End:** This word refers to the end of a cord that is responsible for all movement during the knot's construction. It is the p opposite of a "standing end," which is immobile.

- **Holding Cord:** It refers to one or more cords that serve to secure and maintain the knots formed by working cords. In old patterns, this is sometimes referred to as the knot carrier.

- **Braided Cord:** A material made up of separate threads that are braided together to form the cord.

- **Crown knot:** A beautiful knot that is occasionally referred to as the Chinese flower or Shamrock knot due to its flower-like appearance when completed.

- **Diagonal:** A row or cord of knots that run diagonally from left to right (or vice versa). Knots with diagonal lengths, such as half hitch knots, are frequently employed in these types of macramé designs.

- **Gusset:** A term used to describe the design of the sides of a three-dimensional object, such as a bag.

- **Hitch:** A group of knots that are used to secure an item, such as a ring or dowel. Additionally, they can be linked to holding cables. The Double Half Hitch is the most frequently used.

- **Alternating Square Knots:** This is one of the most frequently encountered terms in Macramé patterns. These Knots are utilized in a variety of designs.

- **Interlace:** It's a design in which cords are intertwined and woven together to.

- **Finishing knot:** A knot used to secure the ends of cords and prevent them from unraveling.

- **Knotting cord:** The string that is utilized to create the design's knots.

- **Folding:** This word is frequently used in reference to Macramé. When requested to wrap a cord around the other, you bend the cord and then invert it.

- **Micro-Macramé:** This word refers to crafts constructed with extremely fine cord materials measuring no more than 2 mm in diameter.

- **Fringe:** Unraveling or beading the cords' ends is a finishing technique. Cords that have been untangled and can either be brushed flat or left wavy.

- **Loop:** This is a critical term in the Macramé lexicon. Crossing one section over another to produce an oval or circular loop (crossing point).

- **Mounting Knot:** A type of knot utilized throughout the installation process. The most widely used is the Double Half Hitch.

- **Picot Mounts:** These are made by folding the cords into loops and sewing them together. Then, they're connected to DHH.

1.3 Macramé Supplies

Macramé does not require any difficult tools or pricey materials. For the majority of projects, you will simply require the following:

- Measuring tape
- Scissors
- Rope

Macramé can be constructed with a variety of cords: linen, cotton, hemp, leather, jute, or wool.

Certain projects will require the use of specialized hardware, such as metal hoops, handbag handles, hardwood rings, and belt buckles.

Additional decorative features, such as wood or glass beads, can be added.

1.4 Best Rope for Macramé

Cotton rope or twine is the best sort of cord for Macramé. It is a soft, flexible material that is readily available. It's simple to knot and will not stretch with time.

Cotton rope can be bought online or at most craft stores. I like to use a 4–6 mm 3-ply cotton cord for the majority of home decor tasks.

Choose a string with a diameter of less than 2 mm for jewelry creations (micro-Macramé).

1.5 Other Materials

You can also use hemp rope or jute to lend your products a more rustic, natural appearance. Although these materials are significantly more difficult to work with, they result in a more textured and durable finished product.

You can also use nylon paracord, leather cord, or polypropylene rope.

1.6 Setting up Your Workspace

Before you begin a new project, you'll want to create a Macramé workstation. Make sure that you have adequate illumination and sufficient space to move about comfortably.

You can work horizontally on a flat table or vertically on a hanging rig, depending on the size and type of your project.

Vertical Setup

Larger projects, particularly wall hangings, will require a vertical workspace. Suspend your work at a height that allows you to work comfortably.

Methods for hanging your item include the following:

- Suspend from a wooden dowel rod hung from a clothes rack.
- Affixed to the back of a door.
- Suspended from the back of a high chair.
- Through the use of a doorknob.

If you're going to be creating a lot of wall art, I strongly advise you to invest in a rolling clothes rack.

Horizontal Setup

On a horizontal, flat surface—such as a table—you can complete certain smaller projects. Secure the piece's beginning end to the table to maintain strain on the cables as you work. You can use smaller pieces, such as Macramé bracelets or the clasp of a clip-board.

CHAPTER 2:

MACRAMÉ BASICS

2.1 Basic Tools

The necessary equipment and tools to begin with Macramé are few and straightforward:

- Mounting cords
- Project board or Macramé board
- Rings for securing the mounting cords
- Pins/T-pins
- A measuring tape
- Scissors
- Beads Embroidery needle
- Cording
- Crochet hook

The Macramé board is the work surface on which you secure your work. A Macramé board can be bought at a craft store. If the stores in your area do not offer Macramé boards, you can get one from our prior post's list of Macramé supplies vendors.

T-pins (alternatively called "wig" pins) are available at most sewing and craft stores. You may also want to buy U-pins, which are excellent for securing heavier cords to the Macramé board. U-pins are available in stores that sell materials for upholstery projects.

You'll use the crochet hook or embroidery needle for projects that require more delicate details.

2.2 Starter Macramé Tool Kit

Fringe Comb

When it comes to creating a lovely fringe for your Macramé piece, I suggest unraveling your threads with a strong steel comb. Another excellent solution that I've seen people frequently use while combing out their fringes is using a specialized pet brush.

When creating feathers and/or a firmer fringe, I suggest using a Fabric Stiffening Spray.

Craft Scissors

Because you'll be trimming and cutting threads very frequently while working on your Macramé creation, I suggest investing in a pair of sharp scissors.

Precision Tweezers and Crochet Hooks

When working with tiny cords and making Macramé jewelry, crochet hooks are indispensable for pulling threads through little loops.

They're also really useful for securing your work, for example, the bottoms of your Macramé bags.

When unraveling knots or making adjustments to your work, it's essential to use precision tweezers. This protects the threads and also makes it much easier to fix any mistakes.

Rotary Cutter

Are you looking for a convenient instrument to assist you in more precisely cutting your Macramé cords? Invest in a Rotary Cutter!

You may quickly and easily cut your fringes and feathers with a rotary cutter.

2.3 Small Macramé Workstation

Discover how to set up a Macramé workstation for little tasks like coasters and earrings.

Macramé Board

Macramé boards are extremely convenient for working on little projects such as bookmarks or jewelry. The cleverly constructed notches on all sides lock your cord in place without the use of pins. Thanks to the boards' lightweight construction, you can take them with you everywhere you go!

Corkboard

Corkboards are ideal for Macramé because they allow you to attach your work with pins, which is especially handy when working on tiny projects like Macramé jewelry or a Macramé purse.

Even though any corkboard will work, it is preferable to use one that has been wrapped in plastic to ensure that no cork residue remains in your Macramé work.

T-Pins

To secure your project to a board, you can use any pin, although I recommend T-pins because of the little handle on top, which make it easier to hold the cords in place.

2.4 Vertical Macramé Workstation

Learn how to construct the ideal vertical Macramé workstation for larger projects such as planters and wall hangings.

Macramé Work Stand

The majority of fiber artists hang their works on a simple movable clothing rack. When used in conjunction with some large elastic bands and S-hooks to secure the hooks in place, you can easily alter the height of your workspace to accommodate different stages of your project.

Large S-hooks

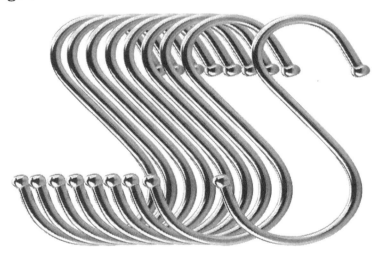

To attach your dowel to the garment rack, you'll need several large S-hooks.

Tip: If the wood or dowel is still too thick for the S-hooks, you can tie your work to the clothes rack using string. This method is even better for non-straight pieces of wood, as you can alter the cord's length by tying knots of varying heights.

2.5 Storage

Macramé Basket

When I'm in search of inspiration for a new project, my favorite thing to do is peruse my Macramé basket. It's brimming with exquisite ropes, driftwood, wooden rings, and gemstones, as well as anything else I could possibly need for a crafty Sunday.

Keep a jar stocked with all unused cords from past projects within the basket. I always encourage storing these because, believe me, you will need them!

2.6 Macramé Projects

Once you've mastered the fundamental knots, there are plenty of amazing projects you can create with Macramé.

Here are some ideas:

Beginner

- Necklace
- Mouse or small animal
- Wall hanging
- Belt
- Simple plant hanger
- Bracelet
- Place mat

Intermediate Projects

- Candle holder
- Collar
- Purse
- Belt
- Wall hanging
- Plant hanger
- Project of your choice
- Pillow
- Animals
- Place mat

Advanced Projects

- Lamp shade
- Large wall hanging
- Window treatment
- Hanging table
- Hanging shelf
- Lawn chair
- Project of your choice

- Hammock

2.7 Get Started with Macramé

The simplest way to get started with Macramé is to choose an easy starter project, such as a plant holder or tiny wall hanging.

It can be challenging to figure out d how to properly measure Macramé strands for a project as a beginner. You can easily avoid making mistakes and wasting your supplies by simply following a step-by-step tutorial.

Learning to Macramé by watching someone else do it, with the additional benefit of pausing or slowing down the video, is the ideal way to get started, and you'll be astonished at how quickly you pick up on the basic knots.

2.8 Practice and Be Patient

Before you begin your project, I recommend practicing funda-mental knots with some of your Macramé cords.

It will take some practice to determine the right way to hold and loop your cords, as well as where to lay your fingers. If you keep practicing, things will get quicker and easier. It's similar to learning to play an instrument; therefore, patience is essential here.

Keep in mind that you will probably get frustrated and make mistakes, especially at first.

With Macramé, you can just untie your knots and start over. Nobody will ever know!

2.9 Types of Macramé Cord

Macramé stores online typically offer three different types of cords: single twist, three-ply, and braided. These cords are available in thicknesses ranging from 1.5 mm to 9 mm.

Single Twist Cords: The cotton fibers are twisted together to create the Single Twist Cords. Single twist Cords are prone to unraveling and are delicate, making them unsuitable for learning knots. They're simple to comb out into a beautiful fringe.

Triple Twist Ropes (3-ply): Triple Twist Ropes are constructed by spiraling three different single-twisted threads. 3-Ply cords are ideal for beginners and are used during practice sessions because of their robust but flexible nature. They create a curly fringe when brushed out.

Braided Cords: While braided cords look stunning in any project, they are not suited for creating fringes. Because of their flexible nature, they may be a little more difficult to work with for beginners.

The kind of cords you use for your creation depends on the pattern, the size of your work, personal preference, and whether or not you want to make a fringe.

2.10 Best Macramé Cords for Beginners

I suggest using Bobbiny 3-Ply Macramé cords while you are still mastering knots and might make mistakes in your patterns.

3-ply cords do not unravel easily, and their solid construction makes practicing your technique, particularly the double half hitch knot, easier.

Thanks to their slower unraveling speed, 3-Ply cords are also better suited for bigger Macramé projects. Remember to always tape the ends of 3-Ply cords when using them.

CHAPTER 3:
TIPS AND TRICKS

3.1 Knots and Techniques

Lark's Head Knot

- The Lark's Head Knot is commonly used to secure cords to a ring or dowel.

- Create a loop by folding one cord in half.

- Arrange the folded cord on the work surface with the loop facing down/towards you and the ends sticking up.

- Bring the loop over the ring or dowel.

- Bring the rope ends through the loop, then tighten by pulling down.

Double Half Hitch

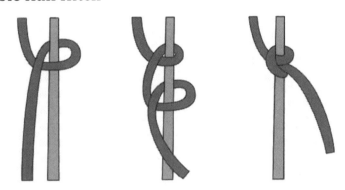

This knot is composed of two consecutive half hitch knots. This is sometimes referred to as a "Clove Hitch." All of the Half Hitch knot variations shown below can be done as a double half-hitch by repeating the processes.

Half Hitch Knots

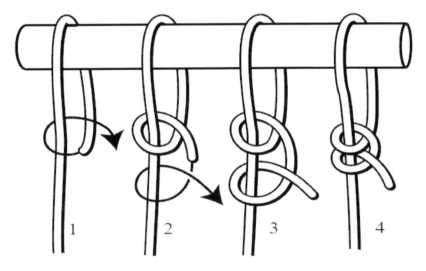

This Knot has many variations. It can be done horizontally, vertically, or diagonally to achieve many different effects. Half Hitch Knots can be tied from left to right or right to left. Due to the simplicity and flexibility of this knot, it is one of the most frequently used Macramé knots.

Horizontal Half Hitch (Right to Left)

Simply follow the instructions above, using the right-most cord as the knot-bearing cord and the next chord to the left as the knotting cord.

Horizontal Half Hitch (Left to Right)

Use the cord on the left to be the knot-bearer and the cord on the right as the knotting cord. The cords used for each purpose vary according to design, but they should be specified in your project guidelines.

Diagonal Half Hitch (Left to Right)

The Diagonal Half Hitch is almost identical to the Horizontal Half Hitch, except that the knot-bearing cord is held diagonally before tying the knots.

Diagonal Half Hitch (Right to Left)

To tie this hitch from right to left, simply swap the knot-bearing cord for the knotting cord.

Vertical Double Half Hitch (Left to Right)

Usually, the vertical double half hitch is formed by working back and forth across multiple knot-bearing strands with a single, long knotting thread. A series of vertical half hitch knots creates thick rows of vertical knots, which is ideal for wall hangings and other projects that require a dense fabric. This technique is a wonderful way to add a splash of color to a project.

- Start with the knotting cord behind the knot-bearing cord, with a short end on one side and a longer end on the other.
- Bring the long end of the knotting cord up and over the knot-bearing cord to the left.

- Wrap the knotting cord's long end around the knot-bearing cord's back and thread it through the gap between the 2 cords.
- Repeat steps 2 and 3 to finish the vertical double half hitch.

Vertical Double Half Hitch (Right to Left)

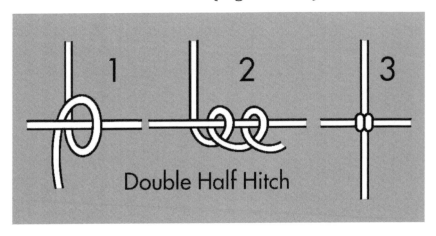

Simply follow the instructions above, starting with the short end of the knotting cord on the right and the long end on the left.

Overhand Knot

This is a pretty typical everyday knot that you have most likely tied 100 times without realizing it had a name! It's an excellent knot to use to secure cords for plant holders or at the tip of a plait/braid.

- Fold the cord into a loop.

- Make a smaller loop near the tips.

- Pull the tips of the cord up and through the loop.

- Secure the cord by tightening both ends.

Reverse Lark's Head Knot

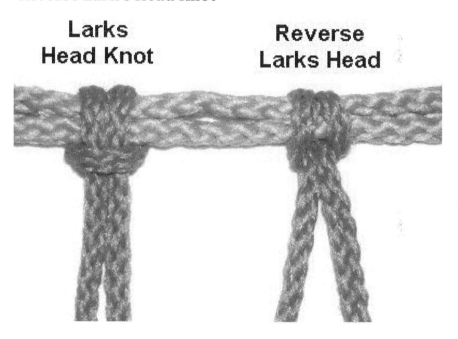

The Reverse Lark's Head knot or cow hitch knot is just the Lark's Head knot reversed. Given that these two knots are virtually identical, deciding whether to use the Lark's Head or the Reverse Lark's Head is purely a question of personal preference.

- Fold one cord.

- Arrange the folded rope on the work surface with the loop facing up and the ends facing down.

- Bring the loop over the ring/dowel.
- Draw the cable ends up and into the loop, then tighten by pulling it down.

Square Knot

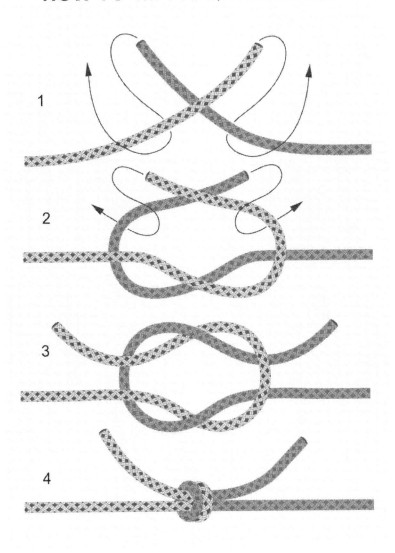

HOW TO TIE A SQUARE KNOT

Square Knots are an extension of the Half Knot (The term "half" refers to the square's half.) You begin by tying a half knot and then complete the square by tying another half knot with the opposite strands.

- Take the right knotting cord to the left, below the left knotting cord, and over the two knot-bearing cords.
- Cross the left knotting cord across the right knotting cord, passing underneath the two knot-bearing cords.
- To secure, pull the knotting cords.

Half Knot

Half Knots are frequently used to form a sinnet. A spiral formed by a sennit of Half Knots is frequently utilized in plant hanger projects.

Four cords are used to work the Half Knot. The outer two cords are used for knotting, while the two core cords are used for knot bearing.

- Pull the left knotting cord to the right, underneath the right knotting cord, and over the two knot-bearing cords.
- Cross the right knotting cord over the left knotting cord and under the 2 knot-bearing cords.
- Tighten the knot by pulling on the knotting cords.

Gathering Knot

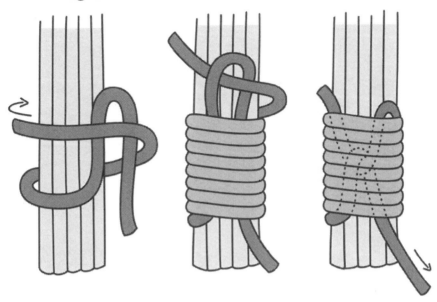

A Gathering Knot is a clean and beautiful method for gathering multiple cords together. This knot is frequently used at the start or at the end of a plant hanger. The knotting cord is a small piece of cord, while the knot-bearing cords are many or even all of the cords in a project.

- Create a loop near one of the knotting cord's ends.
- Set the loop on over the knot-bearing cords, with the loop facing upward and the cord's short end facing downward.
- Keeping the loop in place, twist the long end of the knotting cord firmly around the knot-carrying cords, starting at the bottom and working your way up to the required length, leaving the top of the loop visible above the wraps.
- Thread the end of the knotting cord through the loop at the top of the wrap.
- Pull the knotting cord's bottom end to bring the loop down into the wrap.
- Trim exposed knotting cord ends close to the wrap.

3.2 Tips for Measuring, Selecting and Knotting Your Macramé Cords

In this section, you will learn how to choose the proper type of Macramé cord, how to determine the required length of cord to use, and how to correctly tie the knots in order to produce the desired pattern. A design that contains extremely tight or extremely loose cords or knots would affect the overall appearance of the final product.

If you've ever had a problem with running out of a cord to work with or having an excess of a chord, you'll understand how important these guidelines are. Most importantly, while choosing a Macramé cord, it is necessary to select a suitable thickness, as this is an important component to consider. A thicker cord, as well as a pattern with multiple knots, requires a longer cord.

If you choose a cord type that is not specified in the design, you run the risk of not accomplishing or ruining the project. However, you can swap t different types of cords as long as the t number, diameter, flexibility, texture, and strength are right for that pattern/design.

If you choose to use a thicker cord than the one specified in the design, keep in mind that you will need to make fewer knots than those instructions because a larger cord and more knots make the piece bulkier.

Additionally, when tying your knots, you should be cautious of your surroundings. Consistency is essential while designing a pattern for clothing. The tendency for cords that are extremely tightly knotted to clump is to become tangled. They are not in the proper place to have the desired effect.

On the other hand, if you run out of cord, which happens to the best of us from time to time, you may always revert to the splicing method. When you need to stretch a chord quickly, you can cut it in half lengthwise, unwind it and cover the threads with strong, clear glue. Twist them together and set them aside to dry naturally.

In general, the length of your Macramé cord should be around four times the length of the project. Make two strands out of your cord after it has been folded in half with a Lark's Head Knot. Multiply the length of those cords by eight times.

When measuring the length of your cord, it's important to first consider the pattern:

- If your pattern has many knots, you will almost certainly want an additional rope.
- If your pattern contains many straight cords, you can shorten the rope slightly.
- The greater the thickness of the cord, the longer it must be.
- Braided and three-ply ropes require more length per knot than a single-strand cord.
- When in doubt, cut more rope than you believe you require.
- Always add enough rope at the end to create a fringe (if the pattern requires it).

Other Tips:

If you choose a different rope width from the size specified in the pattern, you must subtract or add length.

- The cord's thickness is specified in millimeters (mm). When choosing the appropriate rope diameter for your project, I suggest using a typical medium-sized cord with at least 3–5 mm diameter. Most fiber artists like medium-sized cords because they are ideal for wall hangings, plant hangers, and other decor projects.

- If you're designing a massive wall installation, you can also go up to an 8 mm diameter. Just keep in mind that using a thicker cord will result in a heavier project.

- I suggest staying under 2 mm in diameter for little items such as bracelets. I recommend making a record of all your cord sizes and type measurements in mm for future reference.

- To be more precise, you can compare the size of each knot individually. Just tie the knot and use a pen to mark its top and bottom on the rope.

- Now untie the knot to measure the amount of cord required for it, then multiply the length of each knot by how many times they are used in the pattern to determine the total length of your project. The majority of fiber artists choose to work with a good quality cotton rope because it is sturdy and resilient and enhances the appearance of their crafts. Cotton rope is extremely easy to unwind, allowing you to create a gorgeous fringe Cotton rope is typically offered in three different configurations: braided, single strand, and twisted. Braided cotton rope is made up of six strands (or more) of cotton rope braided together to form a single rope. Twisted cotton rope is made up of three strands (sometimes known as three-ply) of cotton rope twisted together.

- Certain knots deplete different cords at varying rates. For instance, a lengthy series of square knots will consume far more knotting cords than core cords. Knotting cords should be at least five or six times the length of the finished project, whereas core cords should be no more than double the final length.

- If the design incorporates both open and closed sections, the cord should be approximately four times the piece's final length. The length of the finished piece is determined by the length of cord needed for each type of knot, multiplied by the number of times it is used in the pattern. Chose a good quality rope for your projects. You want a string that is easy to handle, especially as a beginner. If you're just getting started with this craft, I suggest choosing designs that use at least 4 mm ropes to make unraveling easier if you make mistakes.

- If the pattern uses double strands that are folded in half to make two cords, their length should be nearly eight times the piece's final length.

- Depending on the type of knots, thick cords will have to be longer than thin cords. (Knots constructed with stronger or thicker cords need more length).

- If the piece contains many loose sections, you should use shorter cords. If the project is tight and has many knots, you will need longer ropes.

- Always allow a little extra length at the end of a piece to close it off and a little more if you're adding fringes or other ornamental finishes.

3.3 How to Add a Fringe to a Macramé Project

- The kind of fringe you can make depends on the cord used in the craft:

1. Trim the cords to the length you choose.
2. Brush the cords with a firm wire brush, beginning at the ends and moving up (Brushing the cords apart creates a beautiful fringe).
3. Using sharp scissors, trim the ends again.

3.4 Untying Supplies You May Need

- 4 mm Single Strand (Extra Soft)
- Yarn Needle
- Needle
- Appliers

Tips

- Stay Calm
- Dig down into the knot
- Untangle the Knot
- Free the tail
- Proceed one knot at a time

CHAPTER 4:
DIY PROJECTS

4.1 Macramé Jewelry

Macramé Wrap Bracelet

Supplies needed:

- 0.55 mm natural Hemp Twine Bead Cord.
- Sterling Silver Seamless Round Beads 3 mm.
- Awareness Ribbon 11x8 mm, Sterling Silver Message Bead.
- Industrial Strength Glue Adhesive.

Instructions:

- To begin, cut two strands of hemp twine with a diameter of 0.7 mm, one 3' and one 10' in length.
- Cut a length of rope (3') in half, twice its length. Once the folded piece is finished, center the bigger length of twine about an inch from the folded piece's end and tie a Macramé square knot.

- A total of eight square knots are formed by adding seven more square knots to the previous total. Afterward, place a 3 mm sterling silver bead onto each of the two middle strands up to the point of knotting.

- Continue by tying eight square knots and then connecting a bead to each knot until your bracelet has seven beads in total. Once you've completed the first eight square knots, you can add a sterling silver message bead to finish it off.

- Make another set of eight square knots, and then repeat the knotting/round bead pattern from the first half of the bracelet for the second half of the bracelet. The knot in a section of the bracelet when you've finished the second part of your project!

- Using the longer threads on the back of your product, tie a knot in them and secure it with a dab of adhesive. Once the glue has dried, trim the threads close to the knot, being careful not to damage the strands that functioned as the center cords throughout the Macramé knotting process. Once the glue has dried, trim the threads close to the knot.

- Reducing the length of the center cords to approximately 4 inches is recommended. Each of them should have a spherical bead and an overhand knot near the end of their lengths.

- Allow for a minimum of twenty-four hours of drying time before putting on the earrings.

- The bracelet is closed by bringing one of the hanging cords through the loop that has been created by wrapping it twice around the wrist.

Half-Moon Tassel Embellishments

Supplies needed:

- Wooden half-moons
- 4 mm Macramé yarn of your favorite color
- Comb

- Drill bit and Dremel
- Sharp scissors
- Pencil
- Accessories of your choice
- Yarn and needle

Instructions:

- To begin, mark the half-moons with the locations of the nine holes on each half-moon.
- Draw a line through the center and outer edges first, then fill in the rest of the lines to ensure even positioning.
- After that, drill the holes in the wall. Placing a scrap of wood beneath the pieces will help to protect the surface beneath them from damage. Drilling with the Dremel was a breeze, and the wood did not split as it sometimes does when using a drill.
- Next, cut the Macramé yarn into pieces with a sharp knife. Again, Macramé yarn is a good choice because it is inexpensive and simple to work with. You could, on the other hand, use a different type of yarn.
- For every half-moon, you will need to cut 18 five-inch lengths of yarn because each tassel requires two 5" inch lengths of yarn, and there are nine tassels in each half-moon.
- Separate each strand of thread into its own separate piece of thread.
- Use fewer strands after unraveling if you want thinner-looking tassels.
- Comb the two strands of unraveling Macramé yarn together.
- Using some unraveling yarn from another scrap piece, tie off the tassel in the center of the 5" inch sections.
- Tie the tassel top to one of the holes in the half-moon wood piece and knot it in place.

- Trim the ends so that they are close to, but not too close to, the knot.

- This method should be repeated eight more times to complete the half-moon tassel accent, but be sure to keep the tied ends on the same side to guarantee the opposing side is clean and free of knots.

- In the end, all of the tassels will be reduced to two inches on all sides.

- When you are finished, use a needle and thread to attach half-moon tassel ornaments to the lampshades or baskets in the same manner that you would like an ordinary button.

- Make certain that the beautiful side is facing out and clearly seen without the knots.

Knot Bracelet

Materials needed:

- Scissors
- Fabric stiffener
- Comb
- Clothing pins
- Toothpicks
- Two black and ivory 4 mm Macramé cords (choose the color of your choice)
- Measuring tape
- Wax cord or Macramé cord
- Clear, strong craft glue

Instructions:

- Cut a 120-inch length of black Macramé cord in half. It will almost certainly be a little longer in the end, but it is better to be cautious than sorry.

- Then you're left with two 120-inch sections. One will be used to tie the bracelet, and the other will be used to measure the circumference of your wrist. To be cautious, add around 20 inches to the wrist measurement and carefully cut a piece of that size from the remaining 120-inch long piece.

- Tape the component to a solid surface. Additionally, tie the ends of each divided Macramé strand to prevent fraying.

- Cut 4-inch lengths of ivory Macramé cord. Require approximately 25 of them, but again this depends on the size of your wrist. You can even make more cuts as you go.

- Begin with a knot approximately 10-12 inches from the beginning, as you will need a long section to add a tassel to at the end.

- Fold the string's left side over the central string.

- Loop the right side behind the left and center strings.

- Tighten everything up for the initial knot.

- Then, exactly like you did previously, begin with the right thread wrapped over the center strand and the left string looped behind.

- Add a piece of the four-inch Macramé cord to the loop before tightening everything.

- Then you must repeat the knots. The left string is folded over, and the right string is looped behind.

- When I'm tying the square knot, I'm constantly saying "left-over middle string" and "right over the center string with a fringe piece in."

- Continue making square knots and adding fringe until the size of your wrist circumference is attained.

- At the end of the fringe section, you can either finish the square knot with the other square knot or glue it.

- Begin by creating a U-shaped loop at the top and tightly wrapping the cord around it from top to bottom.

- Then thread the cord thru the remaining exposed loop and pull on the lower thread until the loop and upper string vanish beneath the wrapped rope.
- Trim the remainder of the ends.
- Then, as seen in the video, open up and unwind all of the fringes. When they are all opened, straighten them out and trim them to a length of about two inches or whatever you prefer.

Including the Bracelet's Adjustable Closure

- Adjust the bracelet using the sliding square knots indicated previously.
- The bracelet should be crossed.
- Then, repeat the square knots over the two bracelet end pieces in the same manner as you did at the beginning of the bracelet. My string was around 15 inches in length.
- Knot approximately three square knots and was pleased with the result; the bracelet slipped effortlessly over my wrist and was easily tightened.
- To complete it, I tied a single regular knot across the center string, not over it, because you want to avoid glue getting on the center string. This would prevent the closure from sliding.
- Apply some glue to the knot using the tip of a toothpick.
- Assemble the knot securely over the adhesive and cut the ends. If necessary, you may wish to clamp the knot.

Enhancing the Knotted Bracelet with a Tassel

- Tie a knot between the two strings at the point where you desire the tassel to begin. It is approximately 1.5 inches below the fringe portion.

- Unravel three 5-inch ivory Macramé thread strands that I had precut for each tassel. Finish by tying the unraveling parts together.

- Make a double knot and tighten it extremely tight.

- Apply some additional adhesive to this section to ensure the tassel does not open.

- And cut the ends to a length that is not too short.

- Fold and comb the ivory Macramé thread in half.

- Now you must complete the tassel using the gathering-knot procedure as demonstrated previously. If you do not have a wax cord, simply open another length of Macramé string to obtain a thinner piece of rope. However, I adore the wax cord for this and many other projects.

- Cut the tassels to the same length at the end.

- Increasing the stiffness of the fringe.

- Using the fabric stiffener, thoroughly spray the chopped and combed fringe.

- The fringe has a propensity to curl back into the form of the previously twisted Macramé cord. Therefore, once you've sprayed the stiffener into the fringe, continue brushing it until it finishes curling. At times, it can be somewhat defiant, and you may need to weigh it down a little with something. After everything has dried, repeat this technique several times more until the fringe resembled a firm bristle brush texture.

- Trim the fringe as necessary.

- And it is ready.

Macramé Bracelet

Supplies needed:

- Beads
- Lighter/matches

- 0.5 mm cord for knotting
- Scissors

Instructions:

- Begin by cutting two arm lengths of thread and stringing evenly through the stamping blank's holes. These are the intermediate strands. Another arm length should be cut and centered beneath the middle strands. Your left strand and right strand are the 2 halves of this length of rope.

- Begin by crossing the right strand across the middle strands and then under the left strand. Grab the left strand and thread thru the loop you formed. Tighten the knot and slide it up to the stamping blank.

- Complete the knot by reversing and repeating. Pass the left side over the middle strands and beneath the right strand, then pass the right strand through the loop and tighten. Continue knotting right, left and right, left, right until the Macramé is several knots short of the desired length. When you tie the slide closure, you'll add a little extra length.

- On the opposite end of the stamping blank, repeat your knots. Secure the right and left cords with a basic loop and slowly melt the cord with a match to prevent it from unraveling. Trim the extra so that both ends are left with only center strands.

- Turn the bracelet over and align the center strands, modifying the length of the cords to fit comfortably around your wrist. Once you've determined the correct length, use leftover pieces to connect the four stands.

- Cut another long length and begin tying six to ten square knots in an alternating pattern of right and left. Tie off and melt the remaining ends, ensuring that the center strands may be slid to modify the length. Put on your new bracelet with pride!

4.2 Macramé Pillow Cover

Supplies needed:

- Scissors
- Cord made of macramé
- Thread/Sewing Machine (optional)
- Stick or Dowel
- Pillow insert and cover
- Measurement tape

Instructions:

- For this pillowcase, you may utilize an existing pillow cover or build a quick envelope pillow cover. But do not create it until you have completed Step 5. Use this drop cloth to make a pillow cover quickly. It turned up to be an excellent match for the rope and looks great. Choose a cover color that contrasts with the macramé if you want it to stand out.

- The cover is 20x20 inches to provide a sense of proportion. You should double-check that the macramé pattern will suit the pillow, but it's excellent that it can be extended if necessary.

- Eliminate the cords! For this design, you will need sixteen 12-foot wires. (And depending on how long the fringe is desired, you will have a bit more.)

- Secure all 16 cords to the dowel using reverse lark's head knots to learn how to tie this knot, refer to the section on Basic Knots.

- This cover's pattern consists of alternating rows of a single square knot. A reference space of approximately half an inch is left between each knot. In addition, providing a little breathing room expedites the procedure.

- Continue tying square knots alternately until one reaches the bottom of the 20-inch length. Using the measuring tape, keep track of the location.

- After reaching the bottom, make two horizontal rows (left to right, then right to left) or the two times 12 hitch knots.

- After completing the design, trim the excess from the bottom, but leave a few inches of fringe hanging - it is advisable to leave about 5 inches. It is totally up to the user whether or not he leaves a larger tip.

- You may now either remove it from the dowel or snip the end off.

- Here is how to adhere the macramé pattern to the cushion. If you are making your own cover, you will match the pattern to the front of the cover before stitching it together, leaving the cut ends slightly overhanging the top.

- Position the pattern on the front.

- Position the back of the garment on top and attach it with pins!

- Place the back piece on top of the cover and macramé design, right sides together; you are constructing a sandwich with the macramé as the "meat."

- Simply stitch the pillow cover's top seam, including the ropes! It requires some dexterity, but it is possible. One may use pins to hold everything together.

- Insert the macramé pattern into the pillow and sew the other seams as usual to complete the cover.

- Flip it to the appropriate side. The macramé design should now be linked to the cushion's top (emerging from between the seam).

- You can use an additional length of macramé cord to tie a simple knot in the cover's back to secure the remainder of the material. Who is concerned with the back? No one ever sees it. The user can loop this rope in and out of the square knots. This will significantly improve the design and keep it in place as you approach the bottom.

4.3 Clove Hitch Keychain

Supplies needed:

- Beads
- 3/16 inch natural cotton piping cord 1" keyrings
- Scissors
- Floss or yarn for embroidery

Instructions:

- This simple keychain is created by tying two simple knots.
- Begin with two 20-inch cord sections (they can always be trimmed shorter, but it's preferable to start with longer lengths). With a larkspur knot, pass each thread through the keychain, making the outer strands slightly longer than the inner strands.
- Using multiple colors of yarn, create vertical clove hitch stitches. In the first two colors, we completed two rows, and in the third color, we completed one row.
- In the center, create a square knot.
- Create another set of vertical clove hitches by reversing the steps from the previous section.
- It is completed with a quick trim of the ends.

4.4 Christmas Tree Decorations

Supplies needed:

- Cord/string macramé

- Tape masking
- Comb or hairbrush
- Cords Attached to the Twig
- Scissors
- Twigs

Instructions:

- To begin, cut a short branch and tie together six cords using the lark's head knot. We'll use a thread, but we'll untwist it till we've attached it to the little branch and converted it from three plies to one ply. Each rope must be at least 2 feet long. • The subject of how to tie a four-phase head knot for larks arises here. To tie a lark's head knot, bend the rope in half and then place it over the Twig's head in the middle. After bending the circle over the Twig's back, fold it over its upper two ends. There is a significant pull. Rep on every string.

- A small white macramé Christmas ornament with twinkling lights.

- Christmas Square Knot Miniature Macramé Ornament.

- As suggested by its name, the 1st Square Knot consists of a square knot. The initial line will consist of three square knots until the threads are attached to the Twig. Four cords connect the knots, with the first four cords coming from the left and separating them.

- Instructions for tying a square knot for macramé in four simple stages. To create a square knot, draw the knot out of the top left cord in a way resembling the number four.

- The ends of the first chord are then slipped under the fourth chord.

- At the end of the fourth chord, pull up and behind the middle two chords into the gap between the first and second chords that resemble the number four.

- Raise the edges of the first and fourth cords to reinforce and relocate the knot to the tip of the rope. It is the beginning of the square knot.

- The second half of a square knot can be utilized in the same manner but in reverse. You may create the "4" shape for the first and fourth cords, excluding the "4" on the right.

- Pull the first string over the fourth string.

- Next, thread the tail of the first cable through the "4-shaped" hole beneath the second and third cords.

- Pull the edges of the first and fourth cords together to tighten them, and you will have created your first square knot.

- The methods for fastening a square knot in macramé continue to utilize four-cord segments. Connect a unique square knot and then another square knot to create three along the top row.

- In the second step, you will simply tie two square knots. Start by dividing the first one into cords to accomplish this. Row 2 contains the first four cords of the second square knot, followed by another chord. However, it would expose two additional cables.

- To create a square knot, use only the center four cords for the third line.

- If you need to alter the tension, attempt to keep the knots evenly spaced and tightened.

- Macramé with teeny-tiny square knots securing a table

- The fourth row is finished by repeating the second row with two square knots and detaching the two cords from both ends.

- Row five is created by repeating row one with three square knots.

- How is a four-factor half hitch tied? This design may be completed with square knots or a row of half-hitch knots.

- Pull sideways through the piece with the first cord in the row using a half-hitch knot. This is going to be the lead cord.

- Bring the second cable through the created loophole behind and over the first cable. Similar to the first string, tie the second string in a knot. It's only a half hitch.

- Continue along the remainder of the cables, taking care not to flatten the lead cord by pushing it laterally over the wires behind it.

- Pull on the lead line to tighten the knots.

- Four steps for making fringe with small macramé

- To complete the object, cut the ends straight through or make a downward or upward "V" at the base.

- Use a comb or brush to straighten the cord or establish the base for the fringe. After cleaning the object, you may only need to reshape it.

- Finally, to hang the ornament, trim the Twig's edges and connect a length of rope.

4.5 Macramé Banner

Supplies needed:

- Beading (optional)
- Brush made of wire (for fringe)
- 1 7-foot cord and 40 3-foot cords are available in macramé cording.
- Scissors

Instructions:

- This banner is composed of five miniature macramé hangings joined by a long rope. Each wall hanging utilizes eight three-foot cables. To make the banner smaller or larger, simply add or subtract cords.

- To observe its operation, please follow the procedures listed below. You'll quickly get the hang of it!
- Using Larks Head knots, attach eight of the 3-foot cords to the long cord.
- Make three rows of alternately facing square knots.
- With the inner cords of the fourth row, tie two square knots.
- Using the four center cords of the fifth row, tie a square knot.
- Make two rows of diagonal double half hitch knots on either side in the shape of a V. Continue along the same course as the square knots.
- Combine the V shape by tying a square knot with the center strands.
- Cut the excess cables from the underside and use a wire brush to fringe the ends.
- The use of beads to separate each macramé "banner" is entirely optional. Adding a few wooden beads between each banner will do this. Behind the two end beads, one can tie tiny knots to secure them in place.
- As the banner is intended to serve as a focal point in the children's playroom, it may be necessary to clip some excess string from the garland rope. This size worked out great, but if you wish to make the artwork even larger, simply add extra banners.

4.6 Round Coaster

Supplies needed:

- Yarn needles
- Rubber band
- Paper tape for attachment
- Measuring tape

- 24 cords (holding cord 150 cm, 9 cords of 50 cm each, 5 cords of 40 cm each, 11 cords of 75 cm each, 4 cords of 45 cm each, 6 cords of 60 cm each)
- A hair comb
- Baby cotton wool
- Two cardboard sticks which are 3 cm in width
- A pair of scissors
- Scissors

Instructions:

- First, you must form a loop at the end of the holding cord.
- Then, you must fold one of the 75 cm cords in half, position it under the holding cord, and tie a cow hitch knot. This is accomplished by placing the sides of the cord close to the newly formed loop.
- You must now repeat this step three times.
- Next, tighten the retaining cord by pulling it downward.
- Attach the rubber band to the initial string. This will allow you to keep track of the number of rounds you weave with ease.
- Place the holding cord on the right side of the initial string. Move the chord to generate the sensation of the number four. The initial cord should be placed on top of the holding chord. Pull the opposite end of the cord through the newly formed loop.
- Repeat the previous step to create a double half hitch knot.
- Repeat these procedures until your initial string is complete.
- Attach the subsequent string and repeat the preceding procedures.
- Continue adding strings and repeating the instructions until there are eleven rounds.

- When you begin a new string as a beginner craftsman, there will be a gap between the two strings. After completing the eleven rounds, you can fill up the spaces with additional cords.
- Your gorgeous coaster is ready.

4.7 Macramé Hairband

Supplies needed:

- Thin satin ribbon (about 1/8 to 1/4 inch wide)
- 6 colors/12 strands embroidery floss (half wide headband)
- E6000 or a comparable plastic-sticking adhesive
- Matching sewing thread & needle is optional if you wish to stitch the knotted portion on the band to get further stability.
- Half-inch wide headband (or whatever you want)

Instructions:

- Plastic headbands are recommended due to the fact that elastic or knotted headbands do not fit the head and require a full day of reapplication. If you choose a different design, we are confident you can modify this to suit your needs.
- First, make a really long friendship band.
- Use six strands, each of which is ten feet in length, then fold them in half to create five-foot-long strands. However, if the headband is wider, the strands might need to be longer.
- Tie a removable knot to hold the strands of this friendship bracelet together.
- Untie it after you're done.
- Apply a small amount of adhesive to the rear of the band and begin to wrap the ribbon around it. Ensure that the ribbon overlaps on the front and back, and that the attractive side is

facing out if the ribbon is single-faced. Wait a few moments for this to settle before continuing.

- Trim one edge of the tails and adhere it to the strip. Please allow a few minutes for it to settle.
- Apply adhesive to the piece's back and wind the ribbon around it until it is completely coated.
- Continue gluing and wrapping, but this time behind the knotted strip rather than above it.
- Stop gluing and wrapping when you reach the same point by this edge as you did by another when you glued on the knotted strip.
- Trim the ends and join the entire length of the extremely long bracelet to the very end. It is OK that you may need to tug and stretch this a bit to make it fit. (If you wish to stitch across the back of the piece to repair it, simply glue the end.)
- Continue to apply glue to the back and wrap the ribbon around the edge until you reach the end of the band, then connect the ribbon end to the back with care.
- If you have just fused the end, you can now stitch back and forth on the back, catching the piece's edges and pressing it securely into place. Given that the strip's edges are disorganized, this will become an outstanding option.

4.8 Macramé Plant Hanger

Supplies needed:

- Macramé cord
- Metal/wooden ring
- Scissors
- Small plant pot
- Measuring Tape

Instructions:

- The first step is to organize your Macramé workspace.
- Begin by working on a plain work surface, such as a dining room table or a countertop. While tying the initial knots, seal the starting loop using masking tape.
- Once you've knotted the 1st few inches of knots, working vertically will be much easier. You can use a doorknob, coat hook, or clothes rack to hang the planter.
- Cut six 13-foot-long strands of cord if you're beginning the planter with a wood ring.
- If you're tying a loop rather than a ring, you'll need a longer cord than the others. Cut five 13-foot-long cords and one 19-foot-long cord.

After cutting the cables, wrap the ends in masking tape to prevent them from unraveling.

1. Suspend the ring from a hook or secure it to the tabletop.
2. Pass all ropes through the ring. Bring the rope ends together so that they are even on both sides, and the center of the cords lies on the ring.
3. Tie 2 square knots around each of the remaining ten strands using 2 of the outermost ropes.

- To locate the center, fold the 5 shorter ropes in half, and with a piece of tape or a pencil, mark the central point. Fold the ropes in half and arrange them on a table.
- To locate the center, fold the longer rope in half. Wrap the 5 shorter cords in a Lark's Head Knot.
- Tie ten Vertical Lark's Head Knots with a single working cord.
- Flip the cords over after completing the ten Vertical Lark's Head Knots. Make an additional ten vertical Lark's Head Knots in the opposite way using the other working cord.

- At the conclusion, you should have a 7-inch sinnet of knots. To construct a teardrop-shaped loop, bend the knotted section in half. Tie two square knots around the remaining cords using the 2 working cords.

Create a Circle of Square Knots

- Separate the 12 cords into three four-cord clusters. You'll work with a single group at a time. If the cords in each set were numbered from left to right, the functioning cords would be 1 and 4. The filler (inner) wires would be cords 2 and 3.
- Set the other two aside while you are tying knots with the first bunch.
- Tie a sequence (also known as a sinnet) or five square knots with the first group. Rep with the last two-chord groupings.
- This square knot segment should measure 2 inches in length.

Make a Second Square Knot Round

- Lower yourself six inches. Make a series of five square knots. Rep with the remaining two groups.
- The length of this square knot segment should be 2 inches.

Create Square Knots in Alternating Directions

Now we'll go to the basket or "cradle" area of the plant hanger's bottom. Three rounds of alternating square knots will be used in this segment.

- For the first round, go down 2 inches and tie an alternating round of square knots.
- Weave the next round of alternating square knots down two inches.
- Work the 3rd round of alternating square knots down another two inches.

At this time, the plant pot should be inserted into the basket part. The final round of alternating knots should be aligned with the planter's bottom edge. You may need to change the space between the sets of alternating square knots if you're using a smaller or larger pot than mine.

Create a Gathering Knot

- Now we'll create one more section of knots to secure everything.
- Take the pot out of the planter. Calculate the radius of the pot's base (or the distance between the bottom edge and the center point). My pot has a radius of 1.5".
- Reduce this distance by one. Make a spiral of ten half square knots around all remaining cords using the two longest strands.

Create Fringe

- Trim all cords 6–8" below the final knot. If desired, a small dab of glue can be added to the final knot for further security.
- After that, you can create fringe. To begin, unwind the cords using your fingers. Then, using a wire brush, brush the ends to create a fluffier and finer fringe.

Hang It

After completing the plant hanger, it's time to hang it. With a ceiling hook, you may suspend your planter from the ceiling. Alternatively, you can hang the planter from a ceiling plant hook.

Here are some hanging plant care tips:

- Find a stud or joist with a stud finder (wall). Ensure that the hook is screwed into a stud or joist.
- Select a hook screw that is designed to withstand the weight of your suspended plant.

- If no suitable joist or stud is available, use a toggle screw to secure the hook to the ceiling.

Suggestions for Hanging Planters

Here are a few low-maintenance plants ideal for hanging planters.

- Heartleaf Philodendron
- Golden Pothos
- Watering Suspended Plants
- String of Pearls
- String of Hearts
- Spider Plants

Indoor hanging plant watering can be challenging since you don't want water to spill all over the floor. In general, I like to take the pot off the hanger and water the plant well in the sink. I leave the pot in the sink for around 30 minutes to drain any surplus water. Then I dry the pot and reattach it to the hanger.

4.9 Cat Hammock

Supplies needed:

- Wood beads (optional)
- Small clamps (optional)
- Two 18-inch metal hoops
- Scissors
- Round pillow (18-inch)
- Plant hook
- Macramé cord
- Measuring tape

Instructions:

- Make two Vertical Lark's Head Knots using the two brass rings as an optional step. If you don't mind the glistening gold, you can make the process even easier. To attach the Macramé yarn, a drop of hot glue can also be used.
- Make a 40-foot-long piece of thread. That being said, I'm aware that it's quite a bit of reading. When I'm ready to tie the knots, I roll up all of the thread into a nice ball and pull out the extra as I go.
- Start by wrapping the thread around the hoop and tying off the end.
- Wind the yarn neatly.
- Once you have the yarn stretched through the back of the ring and on top of it, draw it to the left side of the ring.
- The cable should then be re-threaded through the loops and up the left.
- When you've finished wrapping, add a few more Vertical Lark's Head Knots to cover up the initial thread.
- In the end, you'll be left with a single length of thread swinging, which you'll cover with the rest of the knots on the hanging cat bed.

- Simply use the same knotting technique I described before to cover the end of your thread and start a new row of knots when you run out of thread while hoop wrapping.

- Use both of the twenty-inch hoops at the same time, saving one for later.

- Macramé DIY cat bed: constructing the hanging component.

- Use the Vertical Lark's Head knots (LHK) to wrap the hoops to form the loop. To wrap the hanging strands in the center with yarn, you'll need around 8 feet of yarn.

- Make sure that you use the right amount of Macramé cord.

- Determine the length of the bed's drop.

- By hanging it from the window, you may get an idea of how long it will be.

- Cut eight equal-length strands of yarn and fold them in half halfway.

- Using a separate eight-foot strand of yarn, tie Vertical LHK in the folded yarn's center after it has been folded in half.

- These knots symbolize the Vertical LHK.

- Use the Gathering Knot Technique to wrap yarn around the strands and secure them with a standard knot.

- However, you can also use spiral knots, nearly identical to square knots, throughout the rest of the job.

- To speed things up and add visual interest, use wooden beads instead of Square Knots in string sections.

- Building the hoop and threading it with yarn.

- Designing the area around the cushion that will serve as a cat bed's lounge area is now complete.

- Make four equal sections of thread and tie them together in square knots on the hoops.

- Make a square knot beneath the hoop to secure the 2 center threads in front of the hoop and the 2 outside threads behind it.

- To fill up the gaps between the top-hung strands, cut a new thread. A Square Knot grid was created by inserting three more strands.

- Cut 24 lengths of 180-inch Macramé yarn. Make an LHK by folding each thread in half and securing it to the hoop.

- The Macramé yarn should be secured to the hoop using Lark's Head Knots, which are made by folding the strands in half.

- Using the Square Knot method, the two LHK per section provide four strands.

- A Square Knot should be utilized to secure each component to the hoop in the same manner as it was done with upper hanging strands.

- To complete the project, repeat this approach a total of twelve times.

- Build a grid for the cat's pillow now, as this is when it will be most useful.

- Gather the two outer strands of two adjacent sections with a Square Knot. Below is a measurement of about two inches.

- After that, continue in this manner all the way around the hoop's perimeter.

- Then, in a crisscross pattern, repeat the previous step. To join the two strands depicted below, a Square Knot is utilized.

- Extra Square Knots are required to attach the second hoop to the first.

- Once you reach the center of the hoop, you can gather the strands and tie them together to simplify things.

- Continue grid knotting with Square Knots.

- Secure the rope strands together in the center using a Macramé yarn knot.

- To assemble the DIY cat bed, attach the pillow to a tassel attached to the base. You've finished the job!

4.10 Boho style

Macramé Table Runner

Supplies needed:

- 12″ wooden dowel
- Scissors
- 3 mm measuring 16″ cotton rope (22 strands)
- 2′ of cotton twine
- Over the door hooks

Instructions:

- Suspend the dowel from the over-the-door hooks after securing each end with a cotton thread. Using a lark's head knot, fasten together the first sixteen feet of rope around the dowel.

- Each 16-foot strand of rope should be attached to another using an LHK until there is 22 total. As a result, you're now in charge of 44 separate threads.

- Put one end of a piece of rope on a door hook and secure the other end with the second piece of rope. You'll use this as the foundation for your next horizontal row of half-hitch knots (HHK). Tie a single knot about 6 inches below the dowel with the second rope coming from the right side.

- Make a second knot with the same thread and place it over the foundation.

- Make certain that their appearance is uniform and consistent.

- Use a half-hitch knot to secure the third and fourth ropes from the outside. You'll begin to detect a pattern. A horizontal half-hitch looks like this.

- Then, all the way across, tie all the additional ropes in a single knot. In order to avoid compressing the breadth of the edges, this should not be too compact.

- Making use of the outside four strands, tie a square knot 1.5" below your horizontal line of knots on the right.

- Make another square knot with strands 9–12 and skip the next four strings (5–8). Continue to skip and tie until you get to the end-point.

- Begin on the right side of the dowel and tie a square knot about 3 inches below the top of the dowel (5 through 8).

- Continue creating square knots using the four strands that have been skipped until the row is finished.

- Pull the right side's two outside strands to the side. Following step 7, make a second horizontal row of knots using the third through sixth strands approximately 11 inches below the first horizontal row formed in step 7. Then, with the remaining four strands, tie another square knot about 1.5" above the previous square knot.

- Continue in the way demonstrated across the entire width.

- The final two strands have little effect.

- In order to produce another horizontal HHK sequence, repeat steps 3–7.

- Tie a second horizontal HHK about 2.5 inches below the first, using the same base strand of rope. This one necessitates that you work from the left to the right.

- A row of square knots should begin on the left, with strands that extend at least 1 inch below the horizontal line of knots being included in each knot row. Then, disregard the first two strands on the left and proceed to tie another entire row of square knots on the right side. An alternating square knot is a name given to this style of knot. There should be a slight gap between these rows so that further square knots can be woven in.

- As many rows of square knots as possible are constructed. Your table runner's focal point will be this part, and everything that follows will reflect what was woven before.

- Another horizontal half-hitch row of knots should be added from the outer left to the inner right.

- For the second horizontal half-hitch set of knots, continue down approximately 2.5″ and use the same foundation rope.

- Using strands 3 through 6, make a square knot using the two outer yarn strands on the right. Strings 7–10 are skipped, while strands 11–14 are used to tie another square knot. Repaint, omitting four strands in a row. The left side will have six strands left.

- Using strands 3–6, tie a square knot approximately 1.5 inches below the final row of square knots on your left side. Skip the next four strands to complete the second row of square knots. These six strands on the right are a product of this procedure.

- The outside four strands on the right side should be used to tie a square knot 11 inches down from the preceding horizontal knot row. The final four square knots should be tied around 1.5″ above the preceding knot.

- The procedure is complete now.

- Make a final row of horizontal HHK 1.5″ below the pattern of alternating square knots. Make sure to take note of the other end's length when trimming. Removing the cotton string from the dowel, gently untangle all of the LHK; after that, trim the LHK loop's ends.

- You'll be able to put up a stunning table today!

Macramé Door Curtain

Supplies needed:

- 3 mm white cotton Macramé string, 3ply twisted
- 36-inch Dowel rod
- Scissors

Instructions:

- This project will require roughly 1400 feet of string (467 yards). Cut 70 20-foot-long strings.
- You can measure the 20 feet using a tape measure or, as I do, by the size of your arm span. Once you've cut the 1st string, use it as a guideline for cutting the remaining strings.
- Utilize a lark head's knot to secure all of the cords to the dowel rod. Your strings should be 30 1/2 inches in length in order to completely cover the entryway when the dowel rod is suspended on the door trim.
- You're going to use square knots to create five triangles across. Each triangle will begin with seven square knots and

taper down to one on the seventh row, using alternating square knots.

- Take note of the various colors of string. Always ensure that you have an adequate supply of the same string brand when working on a project.

- Simply take four strings and wrap two of them around the other two to form a half hitch loop.

- You cannot tie knots all the way across the Macramé door curtain in order for it to divide and allow you to pass through the door or into the cupboard where you hang it. You must begin thinning them out toward the edge.

- I strung 10-inch half hitch loops across the curtain to allow it to be separated and stepped through. Then I began tapering them away from the center, stopping at 20-half inches on each side with the final one.

- You may customize the length of your Macramé door curtain. At 80 inches, cut this one to hang just above the floor. This measurement is necessary if the dowel is to be hung on the door trim.

- You're done!

Macramé Tote Bag

Supplies needed:

- Jute Rope
- Bag Handles

Instructions:

- Cut ten 2.3-meter-long ropes. They can be folded in half and the folded center threaded through the space on the bag handle. Pass the rope's ends through the loop created in the previous step. Tighten your grip. Rep until each bag handle has five pieces of rope attached.

- Separate two sections of rope from one end and push the remainder to the side. With these two parts, we're going to tie the first knot. This is the knot that we will use throughout the instruction, so if you become confused, go to the next several stages.

- Bend the right strand so that it forms a right angle with the left rope.

- Thread the left rope through the gap created by the two ropes. Pull both ends of the yarn apart until the knot forms and is in the proper location. It should be approximately 5 centimeters from the handle.

- To finish the knot, cross the left-hand rope over the right this time.

- This time, weave the right-hand rope thru the gap. Retighten the knot. This concludes the double half hitch knot.

- Utilize the remainder of the strands on the handle to tie four additional of these knots in a row. Then repeat, omitting the 1st rope and knotting the 2nd and 3rd. Carry on along the row. You will tie four knots and leave the 1st, and last ropes untied this time.

- Once the second row is complete, create a third row identical to the first.

- After completing the third row, repeat steps two-four on the second handle. After that, align the two handles so that their rear sides face each other.

- To begin the next row, knot together the two end strands from the front and rear of the bag. Make knots around the front and back of the ropes until you reach the other end. You should now have the last cords on the front and back. Connect these.

- Continue knotting in this style until approximately 10 cm of rope remains on the strands.

- Cut a 4-meter length of rope. Using the same manner as for the handles, attach this to the final side knot.

- Wrap the rope around one strand from the back and one from the front. Tie one double half hitch knot, then repeat with two additional knots. Continue working till you reach the end.

- Untangle the rope that is dangling. To secure, tie strands of this together between knots. You can reinforce these with adhesive. Outline it with a comb to form a fringe.

- And now your bag is complete. If you're looking for something with a splash of color, try dyeing it naturally sage green and burnt red.

Macramé Hanging Pumpkins

Supplies needed:

- Ring
- 7 m Rope
- Pumpkin
- Hook

Instructions:

- Divide the yarn into 4 equal sections and fold them all in half.

- Pass them halfway through your ring and then thread the tails through the rope's loop. This secures the rope to the ring and allows the loose ends to hang down.

- Snip off 2 of the loose ends that are entangled. Knot one of these ropes around the other approximately 20 cm/8" down the rope.

- Repeat this process three more times to create 4 strands of 2 ropes. Bring the two front strands closest together into the center.

- Knot one strand from each strand around the other around 10 cm / 4" from the last knot.

- Take the leftover ropes from these 2 front strands and knot them around the outside two strands' nearest rope.

- On the extreme outside, you will be left with 2 ropes. Wrap one of these strands around the other at the back of the piece.

- Divide the front 2 ropes in half and attach each to an outer rope. Turnover and repeat the procedure on the other side.

- Combine all of the ropes and tie a knot at the base.

- Insert the pumpkin carefully into one of the top gaps. Make an effort not to shift the knots too much while you're doing this.

Camera Strap

Supplies needed:

- Macramé cord
- Industrial strength glue
- Clothespins
- Swivel clasps
- Scissors

Instructions:

- Cut two 4-yard lengths of Macramé cord.
- Fold each piece of cord in half so that one side has 1 yard and the other side has 3 yards. Pass the midpoints of the strands through the flat section of one swivel clasp, maintaining the strands' long ends on the outsides.
- Each cord's ends should be pulled through its loop and tautly wrapped around the clasp.

- Commence by securing a square knot. Cross the leftmost cord (which should be quite long) over the middle two cords and underneath the rightmost (also quite long) cord. Then bring the right cord up and over the left cord, passing beneath the center two. Tighten this. This completes the square knot.

- Make a square knot by repeating step 4 in reverse. Cross the right chord over the center two and underneath the left; then the left cord over the center two and underneath the right. Pull taut to complete the square knot.

- Keep making square knots until the length of your camera strap is comfortable for you.

- All four cords should have their ends trimmed. All four cords should be threaded via another swivel clasp. Apply a dot of glue to the end of each string, then fold the ropes over the clasp and secure them with clothespins while the adhesive dries.

- Undo the clips and reattach the strap to your camera once the adhesive has dried.

Macramé Handles

Supplies needed:

- Scissors
- Purse
- 3 mm natural Macramé string

Instructions:

- Reduce the length of the Macramé string to around 25 feet. You may require more or less based on the size of the handle. These handles measure 5 inches in length.

- If your purse features fabric or leather handles, the length will vary as well.

- Rather than doubling the entire string, fold-down an 18-inch length of a string. The handle is what you will tie the half hitch knot around and so serves as the "filler cord."

- Make certain that the knots are as tight and as near to one another as possible.

- Once you've completely covered the handle, tie both strings in a basic knot and trim the excess.

- Wrap the handle around to conceal the knot at the end, and you're finished!

- If your purse's handles are leather or fabric, you can add a tassel to conceal the finishing knot. That would be quite adorable!

Macramé Wreath

Supplies needed:

- Faux Eucalyptus Stem
- 3 mm Macramé String

- Small Green Zip Ties
- Wooden wreath hoop

Instructions:

- Cut a 15-foot length of 3 mm Macramé string. Utilize a lark's head knot to secure it to your hoop. One of the ropes should be approximately 1' in length, while the other should be approximately 14' in length.
- Wrap the 14' piece of Macramé thread around 1/3 of the hoop using half hitch knots. Bring the cord over the hoop and through the loop you created. Tighten.
- You may have excess string, but it is always best to be prepared than sorry when it comes to string.
- Make certain to draw them snugly.
- Once you're finished wrapping, secure the short length of thread with a half hitch knot. Tie a normal knot as tightly as possible and as close to the hoop as possible.
- Then, using a bobby pin, pass the string through the half hitch knot and trim the extra string so it does not hang down in plain view.
- Utilize zip ties to secure the eucalyptus stem. I picked green in the expectation that they would disappear into the background and become less conspicuous.
- You might use a glue gun to attach it, but this should be done, only if you intend to hang it within the house, not on an outside door. You do not want your adhesive to melt and the eucalyptus to slip off.
- Make a knot as near to the hoop as possible with the large piece of Macramé string. Remove it so that it is not visible.
- Complete the wreath by tying a small piece of Macramé cord around it to serve as a hanger.

Macramé Rope Lights

Supplies needed:

- Cording or Rope
- Small Vessel
- Socket Kit
- Lamp Cord
- Glue

Instructions:

- Begin by fastening the lamp's wire. To keep it stable, you'll want to wrap it around something sturdy, such as a chair back or doorknob.
- Locate the cording's center and secure it beneath the light wire.
- Take the left side and place it over the lamp wire's front and under the cord's right side, making a little loop on the lamp wire's left side.

- Then, using the appropriate rope, secure it behind the lamp wire.

- Pull it completely through the little loop you produced on the light wire's left side. Once you had completed all of my knots, it was time to connect the socket. This can be done before or after you begin knotting; the choice is entirely yours.

- You'll need a cup or planter to make your socket cover. You can take a ceramic planter or wooden bowl; the possibilities are truly endless!

- To begin, drill a hole through the bottom of the cup.

- Then insert the threaded nipple into the socket base (be careful to secure the small screw on the side to prevent the socket from unscrewing while twirling the light bulb!)

- Connect your light wire to the washer, then to the cup, and finally to the socket base.

- Connect the socket in accordance with the specified instructions.

- The washer should then be screwed onto the threaded nipple.

- Slide your rope up and around the tip of the threaded nipple (this is the only modification you will need to make if you connect your socket prior to beginning your knots). Adhere with glue.

- Allow time for the adhesive to dry.

- Your holder is now ready!

Macramé Pot Scrubby

Supplies needed:

- Jute rope (3 mm)
- Scissors

Instructions:

- Cut 12 x 5' bits of jute and tie them with a lark's head knot to a wooden dowel.

- This will result in 24 strings measuring 2 1/2 feet in length.

- Double hitch knots are tied all the way across the length of the first rope on the left side, which serves as your working chord.

- Ensure that they are pulled taut and relatively close to the lark's head knots.

- Begin by tying the first four cords in a square knot on the left side. Continually add square knots across.

- Skip two strings and then tie square knots across the third row. You'll end up with 2 strings.

- Make nine square knots in a row, starting with row 2 and ending with row 3.

- You can undertake additional work if you desire a larger scrubby.

- Tie double half hitch knots onto the 1st string on the left side, using the other strings as your working string across the board.

- After tying the final string on the right, secure it with a basic knot to prevent it from unraveling.

- This is how you will secure your pot scrubby.

- Pull the wooden dowel rod out.

- To hang your scrubby, simply cut through all but one of the strings.

- Trim the fringe on both ends to the desired length. My hair is extremely short in order to minimize shedding. It is non-shedding, which is fantastic!

- That is all! You are now prepared for dish duty!

Macramé Fringe Tassel Pillow

Supplies needed:

- Washable fabric pen
- Plain pillow cover
- Yardstick
- Fabric scissors
- Fabric Glue
- Fray Check
- A decorative fringe trim

Instructions:

- Arrange your basic pillow cover on the bed.
- Then trim the 1st row of fringe trim to fit the pillowcase exactly. There is no need to measure! Simply align them and cut!

- Layout and cut the remainder of your trim rows to length, and spend a little time adjusting them until they look just right on the finished result!

- Using a yardstick or something with a straight edge, join the dots on the edges of where your glue line will be and draw a straight line across... with a pen.

- Pour out an even strip of adhesive over one of your pen lines, following all of the directions on your fabric glue. Then, beginning at one end, carefully press the fringe trim down as you go. It's acceptable if it does not go down perfectly the first time since you will have time to tweak it before the glue dries.

- Maintain a safe distance and check that it is smooth and even, adjusting as required. Then glue the remainder of your rows in the same manner!

- Repeat these processes on the reverse side of your cover to create a mirror image. And don't forget to put the Fray Check on the corners to keep your trim from fraying!

- Although this fabric glue dries quickly to the touch, I waited a solid 24 hours before tampering with it.

Macramé Chair Makeover

Supplies needed:

- Rubber band
- Macramé cord and paracord in similar sizes but different colors
- Flathead screwdriver
- Scissors
- Aluminum chair

Instructions:

- Cut the straps on your chair and then unscrew the posts on the backside of the frame.

- Choose a color and tie a double knot across the frame's seat at the flat front edge. Leave a 5-inch tail.

- To protect my Macramé cord and paracord from becoming too tangled as I wrapped them, I used an elastic band to loosely hold them together.

- Using the central bar at the chair's bend, wrap your rope around the frame and up and over the top. Wrap back under the chair's bend and over the lower edge of the seat structure adjacent to where you began.

- All of your rows must wrap around the frame's edges from front to back. Continue until you want to change the color of the cord or you run out of cord.

- Tie a double knot across the bottom or top frame border, depending on your destination, and leave an extra cord to tuck in when finished. Additionally, as seen below, you can tie onto the following color or strand of cord.

- Weave until you reach the opposite end of the frame's flat section. There will be some negative space in the curved corner, but this is normal. That is how it is supposed to be.

- To begin weaving in the opposite way, simply tie a double knot on the side of the frame and leave about 5″ of a tail. To create the triangular design, place your cord beneath the 1st four rows (2 on top and two on the bottom for a total of four), and then bring it up and over.

- Reintroduce it such that you have 4 remaining on the other end. Wrap your rope over the top of the frame on the opposite side and return the same way you came.

- Wrap around the starting side of your frame and come up beneath those 1st four plus the next two for a total of six skips. Rep the same number on the opposite side and return the same way you came.

- Continue reducing two rows each time you cross, and then return the very same way you came. This will result in the formation of a triangle pattern.

- Continue working with the cord until you reach the end or require an additional end of the same color.

- This is how it seems as the colors change with each additional triangle. For this frame size, I ended up with 3 on the base and 3 on the top. If you're working with an adult-sized chair, I'd recommend using a thicker Macramé string to expedite the process.

- Trim your loosened tails to a length long enough to fold inside and relax. If this were a Macramé craft, your loose ends would be well concealed, but this is a weaving project, and we'll leave the sophisticated knot-tying to someone.

Macramé Hanging Shelf

Supplies needed:

- Scissors
- 26" long wooden dowel
- 178 yards 5 mm cotton rope

- Masking tape
- Wooden shelf
- Wood spacer beads, 17 mm

Instructions:

- Cut thirty-two pieces of 200-inch macramé rope. Masking tape all rope ends to avoid fraying during the knotting operation.
- To create the wall hanging's end straps, tie two sections of rope (each 200 inches long) onto the dowel using Lark's Head Knots, as shown below. It is critical that the outer cords are 140 inches long and the interior strands are 60 inches long.
- Then, make a vertical Half Square Spiral chain. Keep making Half Square Knots until the chain is 21 inches long. After completing the chain, connect two additional ropes and create a 2nd Spiral chain.
- Create two additional similar Half Square Spiral chains using four additional pieces of rope (each 200" in length). Chains or end straps will be fastened to the wooden shelf at each of the four corners.
- Using Lark's Head Knots, attach 24 ropes, each measuring 200 inches, to the center of the dowel. These 100-inch-long ropes will hang straight and evenly.
- Make a horizontal row of Twelve Square Knots just below the 24 Lark's Head Knots, as seen below. Keep in mind that we are only dealing with the 24 sections in the center; for the time being, leave the end straps alone.
- After creating a row of Twelve Square Knots, divide the body into three portions—left, middle, and right. Create 3 Alternating Square Knots underneath the previous four Square Knots using only the left half. Make 2 Alternating Square Knots on the next row. Add a final Alternating Square Knot

beneath those. This results in the formation of a triangle shape.

- Slid a spacer bead onto the center of the two distinct strands at the bottom tip of the triangle. Continue by tying another Square Knot directly below the bead to secure it.

- Create three additional rows of Alternating Square Knots beneath the final Square Knot to construct another triangle shape.

- Continue in this manner, adding additional rows to create a diamond shape. Attach a spacer bead to the diamond's tip. To secure the bead, tie the last Square Knot beneath it.

- Before proceeding with the left section, repeat steps 3 for the right and right middle sections.

- Now, as seen below, link the three parts together by attaching two additional beads. Pass the two inner cords on the diamonds' sides through a spacer bead. Each bead should be secured with a Square Knot.

- Produce three additional little triangles beneath the bottom three beads using Square Knots and the same procedure as previously used to create triangles. Reconnect the three portions with 2 final beads.

- Make a final horizontal row of eight basic knots spaced evenly separated approximately 1 inch below the final two beads.

- Make a Wrapped Tie with the 2 end threads on the left end, immediately underneath the spiral chains. This procedure should be repeated for the 2 end straps on the right.

- A piece of wood roughly 7" x 18" is ideal for the shelf. To begin, sand all rough edges. Following that, I used Liquid Nails to piece them together. Then, using velcro strips, I secured them in place while they dried.

- Then, using a dark stain, stain the shelves.

- Once dried, thread the shelf through the macramé wall hanging's end straps. All cords should be cut to the desired length.

Make sure your macramé hanging shelf is full of plants. You're done!

Macramé Chair

Supplies needed:

- Sandpaper
- 5/8 inch drill bit
- 1/4 inch thick macramé cord (200 yards)
- Drill
- Half inch rope (120 inches)
- Scissors
- Measuring tape
- 5/8 inch hardwood dowels (two)
- 4 1-inch wood screws
- Masking tape
- Saw
- 1 1/4 inch hardwood dowels (3)

Instructions:

- Cut all three 1 1/4 inch dowels to 30 inches in length using your tape measure and hand saw.

- Carefully cut both 5/8 inch dowels to 36 inches in length.

- Put a piece of masking tape the size of one of your 1 ¼-inch dowels. This will assist you in maintaining equal spacing between your holes. Make marks two and three 1/2 inches from the dowel's ends. Replace the first 1 ¼-inch dowel with a 2nd 1 ¼-inch dowel.

- A strip of masking tape should be added to the third 1 ¼-inch dowel. Then, 3 ½-inch from each end, you should make a mark with a ruler. Set this dowel aside; you will not require it until later.

- Discard the masking tape once you're through marking.

- Drill holes where you marked the dowels with your drill. You may like to begin with a smaller drill bit and gradually increase your size until you reach a 5/8 inch drill bit for the final holes. The hole will extend the entire length of the dowel.

- Sand the holes and the ends of the dowels as needed with your sandpaper.

- Parallel the two 1 1/4-inch dowel rods with four holes on a smooth surface. Thread two 5/8-inch dowels along the outside of the holes to form a rectangle frame with four sides. Allow one inch of the tiny dowels to extend from the bottom and top.

- A little pilot hole is all that is needed where the two dowels connect. Secure the two parts together using your wood screws. Rep with the remaining three holes.

- Before you begin working on your macramé, you must hang the frame. For instance, you could use some cord to suspend it from a fence. This is a temporary place and does not have to be the spot where the chair will be hung.

- Cut sixteen 26-foot-long strands of macramé cord.

- Fold one of your macramé cord pieces in half. You can do this by tying a Lark's Head knot by wrapping the cords around the top dowel and drawing them through. Rep with the remaining macramé cord pieces. You now have a total of 32 cords to deal with.

- With the first four cords, tie a left-facing square knot using the two outside cords. A rep for each pair of four ropes, tying square knots. Tighten the knots all the way to the top of the frame.

- Leave the first 2 ropes alone. Make a left-facing square knot using the 3rd, 4th, fifth, 5th and 6th cords. Tying the knots in an offsetting pattern adds security and creates a net-like effect. Repeat the knots across. Maintain a distance of 3 inches between these knots and the row above.

- It is now time for the 3rd row! Make a left-facing square knot with the first four cords. Continue forming square knots until the conclusion is reached. Continue making macramé knots, alternately beginning with the first and third cords. Bear in mind to retain a distance of 3 inches from the row above.

- Continue tying left-facing square knots till your macramé masterpiece reaches a length of 45 inches. It should be positioned beneath the bottom dowel.

- Using a basic knot, tie groups of four cords around the bottom dowel. Secure with a second knot. Tighten these knots as much as possible.

- Measure Twelve inches from the lowest knots of the macramé string and cut across the entire length.

- Cut a 120-inch piece of 1/2-inch rope from the rope. Invert and create a huge loop in the center. This is the loop through which your chair will be suspended.

- Additionally, cut two 65-inch-long strands of rope. These should be set aside.

- The long ends of the rope should be threaded through the two unused holes of the dowel rod on the outside. Allow approximately 20 inches of space between the loop and the dowel. Secure the dowel with basic knots.

- Thread the same bit of rope through the rest holes on the chair's top. Secure with a simple knot. There should be approximately a 30-inch gap between the top of the dowel and the chair used to suspend it. Maintain a loose knot in case it needs to be adjusted later.

- A basic knot can be made with a shorter piece of rope by threading it up through one of the frame's empty holes, starting at the bottom.

- Thread the rope up the hanger dowel until it is completely through. This dowel will be the hanger, so wrap the rope around it and tie a knot, allowing Sixty inches of space between it and the base dowel.

- If you want to hang your macramé chair inside or on a porch, you can use a swinging chair installation kit or a powerful hook to attach it to the ceiling. Outdoors, you can hang it from a branch of a tree. Once the chair is in the desired position, secure all knots.

- Take care when using this chair for the first time! You may discover that you need to alter the knots before using them.

CHAPTER 5:

FREQUENTLY ASKED QUESTIONS

The following are often asked questions by beginners when they first begin to learn Macramé.

Where Did Macramé Come from?

Macramé is believed to originate from the Arabic term "migramah," which means fringe, and alludes to a 13th-century tradition in which Arabic weavers decorated the fringes of horses and camels to keep flies away.

Is Macramé a Simple Craft to Learn?

Yes, Macramé is one of the simplest crafts to pick up! The majority of Macramé designs you see on Pinterest and Instagram are produced with only three fundamental knots.

Once you've mastered these fundamental knots, you can practice incorporating them into various designs. There are simple patterns as well as those that are a little more intricate, which is fantastic since you may continue to challenge yourself for generations to follow!

And the best part is that even if you only learn how to tie a square knot, you can construct an infinite number of various Macramé items, including market bags, wall hangings, and plant hangers.

How Much Rope Will I Require?

It can be difficult to determine the correct amount of cord to purchase. The length is determined by the type and number of knots put on a particular string.

Filler cords, for example, will be smaller than working cords if they include few, if any, knots.

However, as a rule of thumb, allow for 5 or 6 times the length of the task in the cord. If you wish to create fringe at the bottom, add additional length.

Bear in mind that having too much rope is preferable to having too little—you can always clip the excess!

How Many Millimeters of the Cable Would I Require for My Macramé Project?

When choosing the appropriate millimeter cord thickness for your project, the general rule is to use thin cords for little projects and thick cords for large ones.

For instance, when working with thin cords on a big project, please remember that you will need to knot frequently AND that the patterns and knots will be less noticeable.

What Size Cord Should I Use?

The appropriate cord size is determined by the nature of the project. The finer the string, the more intricate the knots.

- For bigger home decor projects such as plant containers and wall hangings, a stronger rope is required. Choose a cord with a diameter of 4 mm-6 mm for these types of crafts.
- For smaller items, such as bracelets and necklaces, use a soft, flexible cord with a diameter of less than 2 mm.
- Consider using a sturdy polypropylene rope for outdoor projects such as hammocks or chairs.

Is Macramé Washable?

YES. Macramé is an extremely strong material that does not disintegrate easily. It may be machine cleaned in a little garment bag at 86°F. Allow to air dry.

What is the Reason for the Unevenness of My Knots?

When beginning Macramé, everyone fights with uneven knots. My most useful advice is to maintain tension throughout the knot-tying process. Strike a balance between too loose (or large) knots and excessively tight knots (too small).

With practice, tidy and neat knots will develop. Continue until your fingers develop a decent beat.

Is It Possible to Use Ordinary Yarn for Macramé?

Despite the fact that you may Macramé with normal yarn as well as jute or hemp, thicker soft-cotton cords are a better choice for beginners to work on.

However, yarn is ideal for low-cost Macramé plant carriers that do not require intricate patterns. Additionally, you can use yarn to make tassels or incorporate it into current Macramé creations like Macraweaves.

Is it Possible to Macramé Using Jute?

YES. Jute and hemp were once quite popular among Macramé artists, but their scarcity on the market led to the development of macramé cords made of nylon, satin rayon, and other manufactured fibers. Nylon or cotton cords are advised for beginners because they are simpler to unwind in the event of an error.

Why Is Macramé Experiencing a Renaissance?

Macramé was extremely popular in the 1970s among hippies but has recently resurfaced as part of the Boho and tribal style trends in home decor.

What Is a Macramé Board?

A Macramé board is used to secure your creation during the knotting process. This can be fashioned from a variety of various materials, but the goal is to provide a solid surface into which pins can be inserted. A piece of polyurethane, a corkboard or 2 pieces of cardboard linked together are all suitable options. T-pins or corsage pins can be inserted into the board without it protruding from the other side.

How Can I Maintain a Uniform Appearance for My Knots?

The easiest technique to ensure uniformity in your knots is to maintain even cord tension and to ensure that each knot aligns up straight on all sides, vertically, horizontally, and diagonally. You'll want to check each knot to ensure that it lines up with the preceding one, that the edges are tight, and that the loops are even, especially when you're just learning. The most effective strategy to ensure that your project is successful is safeguarding it. Larger crafts should be hung from a clothes rack or a stable hook. Ideally, you should suspend your project from 2 locations to prevent it from swinging back and forth. You'll want to create a Macramé board for smaller tasks such as jewelry.

CONCLUSION

Macramé is just one of the many crafts regaining popularity among the fans of DIY, and it's quickly finding its place alongside quilting, surface embroidery, and needlepoint Macramé is a form of textile art that may be used to produce a variety of objects ranging from plant hangers and wall hangings to purses, jewelry, and even garments. It is incredibly versatile and may be used to produce a wide variety of items, from plant hangers and wall hangings to purses, jewelry, and even apparel. Additionally, it is a cinch to learn and can be done by anyone with a little effort. Macramé designs can be as basic or as intricate as the designer chooses, depending on the level of complexity needed by the client. Apart from it, decorative materials such as wooden or glass beads, colorful ribbons, and other embellishments can be used to broaden the design options.

Macramé is simply decorative knot-tying. As with any craft, practice makes perfect, and I think that knowing how to make Macramé is a great addition to your creative arsenal master.

Even though some of the more sophisticated knots take a bit more practice to master, the simple knots demonstrated in the book are enough to get started. This is the beauty of Macramé: even the simplest knots can be used to create breathtakingly gorgeous designs. You can now use them to unleash your creativity with any of the projects in Chapter 4 and make something amazing.

Macramé, which has been a popular decorating technique for decades, adds texture and warmth to a room by tying knots in unconventional combinations to create interesting plant holders, wall hangings, and even a hanging chair. So go ahead and knot away to your heart's content!

Made in the USA
Monee, IL
13 February 2023

27674624R00055